It Doesn't Take A Whole Day...

by Christopher E. Marks

RoseDog❖Books

PITTSBURGH, PENNSYLVANIA 15222

The contents of this work including, but not limited to, the accuracy of events, people, and places depicted; opinions expressed; permission to use previously published materials included; and any advice given or actions advocated are solely the responsibility of the author, who assumes all liability for said work and indemnifies the publisher against any claims stemming from publication of the work.

All Rights Reserved
Copyright © 2007 by Christopher E. Marks
No part of this book may be reproduced or transmitted in any form or by any means, electronic or mechanical, including photocopying, recording, or by any information storage and retrieval system without permission in writing from the author.

ISBN: 978-0-8059-8723-2
Library of Congress Control Number: 2007921081

Printed in the United States of America

First Printing

For information or to order additional books, please write:
RoseDog Books
701 Smithfield St.
Third Floor
Pittsburgh, PA 15222
U.S.A.
1-800-834-1803
www.rosedogbookstore.com

The title of the book "It Doesn't Take a Whole Day..." comes from the complete saying "It Doesn't Take A Whole Day to Recognize Sunshine." This is a phrase that is very meaningful in my opinion. To me, it means that it doesn't take long to realize the truths in life or the truths in individuals. Truths such as honesty, integrity, passion, love, and beauty are easily recognized when you encounter them.

I started writing in April of 2001 following the end of a failed relationship. Writing was my outlet to express the feelings and emotions that I experienced at the time. The poems that I began writing were not of the bad times experienced, but those good times. Those good thoughts and those positive feelings began flooding the pages as I wrote. I guess that's the romantic in me coming through.

As time has passed and my relationship experiences have increased, I have tried to always take those moments and feelings and express them in the form of poetry. I have found that as I have continued to grow, so too has the style and substance of my writing. The poems in this book are a compilation of this journey.

The first selections in this book are the first poems that I have ever written. The three poems, My Queen, That Day, and The Next Step are all interrelated. There is a fourth poem in the collection titled the The Next Step II. This poem was written by a friend and her name is Alima Wheeler. Her poem was the female response to the Next Step. Once you read it, you'll see why it is one of my favorites.

I thank God for this gift, and all my family and friends for being who you are to me. I have to give a special thank you to my God Sister Sharonna Miller for all of her support and motivation. She was the first person to read my work and she has been my editor-in-chief ever since. Thank you so much for all you do. A big thank you to Christopher "CJ" Johnson for his mastery on the book cover and interior artwork. You really made this come to life.

I thank you all for your support and I hope you enjoy the book.

Table of Contents

My Queen 1
That Day 2
The Next Step 4
The Next Step II 6

Music
Tuned In 10
Gentle Stare 11
Let the Music Play 13
Communication 15
Static 16
The Musician 17
The Music 18

Admiration
Portrait 22
Need 25
Your Lips 26
Sleeper 27
Fresh Air 28
Those Jeans 29
Thoughts Untold 30
Precious Things 32
The Beauty of it 34
Mind Design 35
Glimpse of you 36
Again for the first time 37

Memories
Missing you 40
Sight 42
Chapters 43
Edge of Sanity 44
Misdirected 45
Disappointment 46

Table of Contents *cont.*

The Inner Me 47
I Now Realize..48
Pillow Thoughts...49
Heartstrings 50
Since 51
Incense..52
The Fall...54
Mind Blowing...55
Last Night 56

Creativity
Daybreak 60
Circumstance 62
Earth...66
Another Circumstance 68

Love
The Sunrise 74
At Night I Hear A Whisper 75
Soon..76
Unforgettable...77
Impression 78
Good Night..79
Kiss Of A Tear..80
P.E.E.R. 81
Intangible Dreams 82
The Moment...83
So Sensual 85
The Night 87
The Truth 89
Your Light..90
Fantasy Within A Dream 91
Fantasy In A Dream II 93
Just Because...94
Sunset and You 95

My Queen

How can you long for someone that you have never met,
how can you miss someone that you never have seen,
will I know her when I see her, will I know that she is my Queen?
Will I know that this is the woman that will bear my seeds?
Will I know that she is my earth for which I will live and breathe?
Will I know that she is the one that I would give my life,
Will I know that she is and forever will be my wife?
Will my Queen recognize me,
Will she know that I am her King.
will she know that our love will grow like a tree,
bearing branches and fruits for all to see.
Will she know that her mere presence will fill my soul,
with love and admiration and make me whole.
Will she know that I will be her husband, lover, and friend,
will she realize that our love will never end.
As for her smile and her touch it's more of the same....
her touch would soothe the savage beast, her smile could stop the rain.
Will she know that our love will be as pure and innocent as a dove,
will she know that I know she was sent from up above.
Only God could create a creature this pleasing to the eye,
When I see her will I be able to say Hi?
Or will I be intimidated and awestruck by the vision that I have seen,
Will she be thinking the same about me?
Will we recognize each other,
Have we already crossed paths with one another?
Once, twice, maybe even daily,
 how will I know her if she doesn't tell me?
Is this reality or is this a dream?
Could it happen or is this some imaginary scene.
We all know life is more like a wrestling match instead of a dance,
Is our existence based on some pure uncontrollable circumstance?
How can you long for someone that you have never met,
How can you miss someone that you never have seen,
Will I know her when I see her, will I know that she is my queen?

That Day

Going through the normal routine of the day
Trying to excel and trying to make my way
No time to stop and enjoy life at all
Too busy or too tired is always my call
I'm a mere shell of myself operating without a soul
Body and Mind focused in daily cruise control
I take a break to check the scene
I cannot believe what I've just seen
I remove my glasses and wipe my eyes
This can't be real, it's got to be lie
The queen that I've longed for, can this be her?
I've got to get a closer look just to make sure.
As I stand up at my desk my focus has changed
No longer at work only to know her name
Now I begin my approach, approaching from the rear
I am checking her dimensions as I get near
About 5'8 or 5'9 would be my guess
About a size six or seven at best
Long silky black hair cascading down her back
From this angle there are no attributes that she lacks
She has a style and stance that commands respect
If she isn't married she has a man, I'd bet
Lets check her hands and make sure she is not taken
This could be a wasted trip that I'm making
I glance down quickly no rings on either hand
Can this be right this goddess has no man
I'm almost upon here and as I draw near
I am struck by this beautiful aroma in the air
A scent that catches all of my senses at once
A scent that feels like a warm caressing touch
Now I'm upon her, no turning back now.
I must see the face of this beautiful black flower.
As I walk passed her, she turns toward me
I am frozen by the most beautiful woman I have ever seen.
Her complexion is a beautiful shade of brown,
Her eyes are distinctive, sexy, and round,
Her cheek bones are high, her lips are full
This has got to be the most beautiful woman in the world.
And that smile, that smile of hers is easy to describe.
It is bright and full like the sun in the sky.
She has natural beauty like the stars and the moon.

That Day cont.

Her presence alone can fill an empty room.
I catch myself in an imaginative blank stare,
She took her hand and pushed back her hair.
This beautiful queen had to say hello a second time
I missed the first 'cause she was fine as wine.
Now I'm composed and I say "Hi",
I extend my hand looking her square in the eyes,
She takes my hand, she's breathless, then SHE sighs,
"It is a pleasure to meet you, what is your name?"
I told her mine and she did the same.
This was the first meeting of many to come
I know from that first meeting that she was the one.
As we grew and we talked, similarities were abound
I still cannot believe this woman I found.
Or did she find me as I went through my day,
Focused on work and never any play,
That day and that moment changed my life,
That was the day I met my friend, my lover....my wife.

The Next Step

Hey baby how are you today?
That's good, come with me as I have some things to say.
You know we have been together for a while
I love your dialogue, your persona, your smile.
I've thought long and hard about what I want to do
So now please listen to me as I try to tell you
Baby you know I love you, and everything you do
From the way you curl up when you sleep
To how you fuss at me when you keep
Me in line, those times I get a little too charged
Baby, you know you're my Shining Star
I've imagined our lives intertwined in the future
And one thing that I know that will be for sure
Is that my love for you will never diminish
Shhh baby...wait a minute, let me finish
I can remember the first time that you and I met
That's a day that I will never forget
It's funny how only that one sight
Of you, has made such an impact and change in my life
How we have grown and shared so my times
All of those hills and mountains we've climbed
Always together through thick and thin
I love you so much I don't know where to begin
To tell you how much you mean to me
But let me tell you about this vision I see
I see us together for years to come
Because I know in my heart that you're the one
To forever be there by my side
To forever be the apple of my eye
The two of us living in our own home
Our own castle with our own throne
Children born both healthy and strong
Our lives happy, passionate, and long
This vision of us I have longed to see
And It's time to make my vision a reality
Now baby I am going down on one knee
Allow me to take your hand so I can present you this ring
This ring symbolizes all of the ways I feel for you inside
And I would be greatly honored for you to be my bride
To forever love me and be my moon
You as my wife would be my dream come true

The Next Step cont.

I long to wake up to you each and every day
And I promise to love you in each and every way
My goal as your husband will be to fulfill your every need
To support you in anything you choose to be
If you want to leave your career to become a housewife
It won't matter to me as long as you're still in my life
My intentions and sincerity are easy to see
So baby I have to ask you....will you marry me?

The Next Step II
By Alima Wheeler

My Heart is Pounding so Fast
My tongue feels like it's in a cast
Preventing me from Speaking
As happy tears flow down my cheeks
Your confession of love has melted by soul
And pieced my broken heart back together making it new and whole
Your love is like the rain flowing through my body, Indescribable
Like my mouth savoring the taste of beauty
Like the sun when it sets
Like having no regrets
You are my safety net
I knew when we first met
That you were different from all others
So much more than just my lover
So much more than my friend
If obsession is a sin
I'll repent, over and over again
Because I love your dirty drawls
The way you start to argue and then pause
And pretend that I am right
Just to avoid a fight
You let me have the left side of the bed
Speak to my heart without words said
Dry my tears and protect me from harm
You are truly my lucky charm
My Love for you is wider than an Oceans length abound
Your love for me is louder than happiness exceeding sound
I want to spend my life with no one but you
In storms as well as sunny days with skies of blue
In all seasons that shall pass
You will never have to ask
If I will ever leave your side
As you face me with gazing eyes
Presenting this symbol of your feelings inside
Sincerely asking me to be your bride
Looking up from on bended knee
Explaining this beautiful vision you see
Well baby, there is only truth in reality
And the honest truth is............

The Next Step II cont.

.......I want to have your kids
Grow old together
And Make our love last forever
Will I marry you?
My answer could only by YES
For with you, I have truly been blessed
Honored and ready to spend the rest of my life
With you as my husband and me as your wife.

MUSIC IS INSPIRATION ALL WITHIN ITSELF…

Tuned In

I'm tuned in
To your frequency
Can hear your song
When you speak to me
Your sounds are pulsating
Through my emotional speakers
The equalizer in your facial features
Magnifying every pitch of your mood
Making my mind and body
Move
To your intoxicating groove
Please don't change your frequency

Gentle Stare

Is it the smoke
Making me choke
Or love flooding
The atmosphere
Like a fog,
In the mist
Of this room
I can hear you
Speak to me
Inaudible
Your gentle stare
Caressed my soul
Playing the chords
Into soothing harmony
As jazz fills the room
Your heart sings to me
With an elegance and reverence
Only surpassed
By the choirs
Of heaven…
Angel-like
Angelic
Whispers
Cascade from your lips
Enticing me
To hold you,
Mentally, spiritually, emotionally
Firmly, strongly, longly
Until we melt
Into one another's being
This feeling, intensifies
As the piano speaks
So vibrantly aloud
The crowd
Captivated by the musician's
Stage presence
Is unaware
Of the music
Our music
Made in a
Gentle stare.

……Love someone that wants to love you, not someone looking for someone to love….

Let the Music Play

Turning out the lights
To settle down for the night
Music playing
In the background
He goes to turn it off
She asks to let the music play…
Settling down to rest
His arms
Surrounding her
Her head on his chest
His heart
Beats
Her favorite lullaby
So she can rest
He speaks to her softly
To massage
Her soul
His words
Ease her mind
Inebriating her
Like a fine wine
Allowing her
To enjoy the time
She spends with him…
He is her friend
Closer than any friend before
What does this relationship
Have in store?
Neither knows
But they let the music play…
Old crooners
Mixed with R&B
What a sight to see
Opposites
That harmonize
So beautifully
He smiles
As his head sinks
Deeper in the pillow
He is so comfortable
With her

Let the Music Play cont.

As she is
And she is not his
But I'm willing to bet
One day she might be
You see
She may feel the same as he
She is his friend
Closer
Than any friend before
What does this relationship
Have in store
Neither knows
But they let the music play…
Same lyrics
Different styles
Same distance
Different miles
Walking paths
Through different terrain
Love is still love
No matter what music is playing…
He sleeps there
Breathing her air
She sleeps
Cuddled by his love
They rest there
In such a splendid way
They rest there
Just letting the music play…

Communication

I've opened your mind
To my thoughts
Opened your feelings
To my heart
Now we share the same page
Dance on the same stage
Our goals are now aligned
Preparing to merge completely in time
Physically, mentally, emotionally, spiritually
I finally feel that you're hearing me
And now I'm hearing you
Sharing your feelings
Finding your clues
Speaking your words without being said
Completing your sentences within my head
Your heart now beats within mine
Our love has developed like a fine wine
As the time goes on
Our relationship grows strong
Until we reach that priceless perfection
You are my heart's protection
My feelings are in your hands
My love is at your command
And you've opened my mind
To your thoughts
Opened my feelings
To your heart
So that we can now share
The same page
And we can dance together
On the same stage.

Static

There has been static
In your reception
Lately
Your words
Not so clear
Your melody
Hard to hear
Your frequency hasn't changed
But your station no longer
Knows my name
I am now estranged
To the music that I hear
It appears
You're no longer here
Not so appealing
Not so revealing
Just simple and plain
The mode, pitch, and mood
The same
Short
From an artist
With no name
Gone
Without being disclaimed
Once tuned in
Now
No longer friends
Amazing how quick
A melody
Can end
So soon
After
It begins.

The Musician

Approaching his instrument
With a devil's smirk
He mutters "Time for work"
In the nights dim light
Beginning soft and slow
Playing chords you know
A familiar tune
You've danced to
Written on the stanzas
Of his mind
Memorized
But he decides to improvise
Massaging your keys
With closed eyes
It's been a long time
Since you've felt
Creativity's feverish flow
The room fills with your orgasmic tones
Feelings and sounds
You've never revealed aloud
Express the gratitude and joy
For the musician
Who plays your keys.

The Music

From a single beat
And an unheard melody
The Music
Is born...
The beat repeats itself
First unorthodox
Painfully staccato
Until it establishes itself
Finding a rhythmic pattern
Similar to that of a heart
Consistent smooth
Never wavering or changing...
With time
The beat
Transforms and evolves
More creative, complicated,
And dynamic
Into a pattern that more reflects
The mood and personality
Of the music itself
A deep rhythm
Representing the joy
The pain
The strength, the fears
The unknown
Aggressively smooth
Lively yet laid back
Sultry passion
Massaging listeners
Into mindless zombies
Leaving their bodies
Pulsating and gyrating
Uncontrollably
Around the beat...
The music
With the ability
To enhance emotion
Stop rage
And ease a young babe to sleep
The music
Able to paint pictures,

The Music cont.

Heal wounds
And incite a crowd
The music
Timeless
Priceless
Continuous…
The music.

ADMIRATION IS ONE OF THE MOST SINCERE FORMS OF FLATTERY...

Portrait

A still canvas
Was all
That stood
In the beginning
A vision untouched
With so much
Hope and inspiration
Dream and expectation
Manifested glory
In a being just born...
Slowly in time
The canvas began to grow
Learn
And take on a personality
Of her own...
Basic
Primers of love and nurturing
Applied first
Coat her
Completely
To provide her
A background
A foundation
A platform
For continued growth
And development
Through all of life's
Stresses and misfortunes
The vision
Begins to take shape...
Colors
Begin to appear
Almost out of nowhere
Bright, vibrant
Energetic
In a multitude of shades
Colors
The shade of a child's laughter
Mixed with the summer sun
Colors learn to crawl,
Walk, and run

Portrait cont.

Together
Forming unique
Shades and forms
Living and warm
Moving and speaking
On their own
Her personality is
Now clearly defined...
A child with
An inquisitive mind
With trouble
Not far behind
But love, honesty,
And integrity
Are now her cornerstones
She is at home
Even when away
She always seems
To be at play
Even in times
Of great despair
For everyone
She cares
Love now powers her soul
The portrait is now refined...
But still needs to grow
As time continues to move on
She continues to grow strong
Gaining strength
From her mom
And life's stresses
When things go wrong
She is now full grown
The portrait
Is done
completed
Molded, painted
Perfected
Perfectly
To its own unique
Style

Portrait cont.

She makes me smile
As I gaze at her
She is ...
So true to life
So true to love
So true to herself
This is
The portrait of you.

Need

A flower has bloomed
In my soul
For you
A love so true
And unexpected
Cultivated by your touch
Your breath
Provides air
For me to breath
In time
You have become a need
Like water and nourishment
Without you
I feel spent
Tired, sluggish
Inattentive
Missing the love
You give
Impatiently waiting
For your return
So that my heart
Can once again burn
With the flames of passion
Right now
I'm fasting
Savoring the taste of your beauty
Anticipating
When I will see you again.

Your Lips

Soft, supple
As alluring as a bubble
Candy Coated
Transfixed in air
Drawing me near
Wanting to touch
Pressing to feel
Your lips
They have such appeal
Your lips on my mind
From morning till evening time
Whether you're there or not
Your lips I have not forgot
I just want to kiss them one time
Ok, I'm lying
As much and as many times as I can
Let's mass produce them
Sell them by the can
Put them on every shelf
And in every store
One taste of your lips
Will make ALL yearn for more
I love to watch you speak
One day I hope to reach
Out and taste them for myself
Ok, I'm addicted and
I think I need help.

Sleeper

It appears
That many have slept on you'
For years
Many lonely nights
Many lonely tears
But I see through your disguise
Those diamonds in your eyes
Glisten like stars
In the night
It's not right
For you
A priceless jewel
To be
Undiscovered
A not yet uncovered
Resource
Of natural beauty
Any man
Would be a fool
Or just plain blind
Not to recognize
That you're so damn fine
And emotionally sound
You could be
The most heralded gem
Never found
A sleeper
Helplessly lost
In the crowd
So it makes me proud
Knowing
I didn't sleep on you.

Fresh Air

Meeting you
Was like experiencing
An ocean's breeze
On a hot summer's day
Opening my pores
To such new and wonderful things
Refreshing me
Relieving my humidity
By cooling my thoughts
Allowing me to breath
Again.

Those Jeans

Watching you in those jeans, is one of my favorite things
Those blue jeans on your full rich legs, Will make any man beg
Just to see you stroll by again
Those jeans on you, has GOT to be a sin
For what it has done to my imagination
You in those jeans is my greatest temptation.
I watch as they flow over your backside and hips
If you were a drink I would have to take a sip
To get intoxicated off the sight before my eyes
Seeing those jeans hugging your thighs
I'm mesmerized just watching you walk
I'd love to listen if your jeans could talk
To tell me how wonderful it feels when
They are that close to your beautiful brown skin
To move as you move, so silky and so smooth
Scanning over your perfect curves
Leaves me at a loss for words
Just standing there watching, not making a sound
"I swear I didn't know your ass was that round!"
But your jeans have told me the truth behind the scenes
Your body is bangin'. if you know what I mean
But there is one thing that I neglected to mention
How your jeans command so much attention
You hush a crowd when you enter an affair
Heads begin to turn and people begin to stare
At your natural ability and god given graces
With your jeans written all over their faces
If I made a movie, I would make you a star
Your part would be simple and not very hard
No lines to memorize and only one scene
Just walk back and forth in those blue jeans.

Thoughts Untold

I hope you don't mind
If I begin
To tell you what's on my mind
I know you're modest and a little shy
But inner beauty mirroring yours
Is hard to find
And I don't even know you
Really
You may think this is silly
And you may not feel me
But I'm feeling you
It's true
Ask your best friend
She knew
Months ago
For sure
I heard so much about you
Before I met you
From your girl
Telling me about your world
Describing you as
A strong woman
And such a great friend
Some of your accolades
She couldn't even begin
To put into words
And when you responded to my poem
With one of your own
Your creativity, thoughtfulness and beauty
Was clearly shown
And meeting you
Was the icing on the cake
You can't fake
And you can't hide
Behind those chestnut eyes
And that nice smile
I was peeping you
Before I had even seen you
Checking you out
Before your name
Beautiful flower left my mouth

Thoughts Untold cont.

And seeing you
Brought that image into reality
Putting these thoughts on paper
May be a fallacy
But I would rather error
On the side of admiring
Instead of being quiet
And hiding
The impression that you've made
Without even having to say
A word
....
In the future
One day
In a city, at a park, or in a small café
We'll sit and talk
And maybe that will spark
Conversations about you
Conversations about me
Conversations about us
But we'll see
What the future holds
Thoughts expressed
Are better than those untold.

Precious Things

A kind word
A nice gesture
A smile
A hug
Simple
Remarkable
Unforgettable
Often taken for granted
Most important
Many times unspoken
Whispered gently
In a wink
The blink of an eye
The sky
A sunrise
The sunset
Limitless things
Limitless beauty
Immeasurable
A daily portrait
Painted
For you
Of you
In and out
Without a doubt
So precious...

Single
thoughts and explanations
Cannot express
The meaning
The purpose
Of your being
Your touch
Necessary
For so many
To define friendship,
Love, caring and sharing
Non-judgmental
Healing
In your listening

Precious Things cont.

At times
Balancing
The weight
Of your world
And that of others
On your shoulders
Yet
You stand strong
Pressing on
Unable to falter
Showing no signs of stress or strain
When most would have crumbled
Complaining
About having to much pressure
Baby
You are the measure
Of a strong woman
Don't forget that
You are
More appreciated
Than you can comprehend
More loved
Than you could understand
So precious…

Accomplished more
Than some thought you could
Going much further
Than some thought you would
Never ceasing to be that woman
That you are
Maybe
On a clear night sometime
I'll show you your star
As it dances in the night sky
Flickering proudly
As if it were laughing aloud
No cloud
No fog, nor rain shower
Can diminish your star power
Your shine
Always comes through
So precious…
You.

The Beauty of it

You say you're so simple
And wonder why
I see you the way I do
You say it's just my perception
And baby
That might be true
But your beauty is so clear
I have no fear
Telling you my thoughts
I knew that first time
When our conversation sparked
That there was so much more
So much to explore
In you and about you
Through these eyes
You are divine
With no makeup and no disguise
What you see is what you get
You are as good as it gets
You may not be what every man wants
But you are what a true man needs
A strong woman by his side for him to please
I hope I haven't scared you
With some of the thoughts I've expressed
But with you I am truly impressed
You are
Simple but complex
Elaborate yet plain
The beautiful flower
Described in your name
Believe it or not
These things I say are true
The beauty of it all is
That the beauty is you.

Mind Design

With my emotions
As the fabric
My words....the thread
I will stitch a gown for you
From my love...
Sentences form
Attaching my thoughts,
Emotions and feelings
Turning raw, primitive emotions
Of passion and love
Into...Elegant
Sexy, Sultry
Flowing
Majesty
Around your being...
This gown created
Solely for your essence
Accents every portion
Of your magnificence
Each stitch meticulously
And carefully
Placed as
Each thought I have of you...
Mentally stimulating
Emotionally gratifying
And Physically satisfying...
With each step
Your beauty
Intensifies
As your gown forms around you
Until it culminates
Completed
Before me...
You stand here
Draped in my love
You stand here
Draped
In my mind's design.

Glimpse of you

A moment, a minute
In time's space
Echoed by the mark
Beauty left upon your face
A glimpse
Of the heart that resides
In your soul
A glimpse of the truth
In your eyes to unfold
A glimpse of your thoughts
Expressed by your words
A glimpse of your feelings
For others gone unheard
A glimpse of the moment of time
We shared
A glimpse of your song
Replaying in my head
A glimpse of someone
So beautiful and true
A glimpse of a queen
A glimpse of you.

Again for the first time

You're more beautiful
Than I remember
Its been almost
Four years
Since the last time
You truly do age like wine
More stunning and potent
With each day that goes by…
I said "Wow"
Aloud
Countless times
For those 42 hours
You were mine
A weekend…
Such a limited time
For you
To blow my mind
But From the time
Your flight arrived
Till it was time
To kiss goodbye
It was wonderful
Seeing you again
For the first time.

LEAVES FALL LIKE TURNED PAGES IN MY MEMORIES...

Missing you

Thousands of miles
From your touch
My thoughts rush
Back to you
The ocean's
White caps
Draw a map
Of your portrait
Outside my stateroom
The warm ocean air
Is almost
As refreshing as
Your voice caressing me
each morning...
As I stare into
The relenting distance
My heart can't help but mention
How this view
Is almost
As lonely as the sunrise
Without you...
Maybe if I
Throw a penny in the ocean
And make a wish
You will visit
Me in my dreams
To allow me to rest
With you
Tonight
The light
From your eyes
Is all I see
Missing you
Clearly...
Nature can enhance
A feeling
Strengthen a thought
Provide an answer
To questions
An earth old
But

Missing you cont.

It cannot
Make me
Stop…
Thinking of you
Missing you
Can't wait
To get home
To see you
And be with you
Again…
My friend
Missing you
Will soon
Be at an end.

Sight

Somehow
You have trained your eyes
To look
But
You are yet to learn
To see...
The essence of an individual
Not by the outer shell
But by the soul residing within
See past falsehoods
To uncover trueness of friends
See and understand
The necessity of rain
The joy experienced
In the absense of pain
The soothing beauty
Hidden in a smile
The courage and creativity
In possessing one's own style
The importance of love
Whether lost or gained
The pride or respect
Found simply in a name
Life's most treasured things
Don't cost a dime
The greatest gift you can give someone
Is your time
An ounce of love
Weighs more than a pound
Of hate
Only God himself
Has control of fate
The sun does shine
Even on a cloudy day
Blessings come to you
If you would only pray
You must love yourself
Before you can love another
Believe in what's right
And never have to wonder
Truth is sight
So see the truth.

Chapters

Life is a book
As well as a stage
Each triumph, every slip
Written on the page
Chapters are written
From experiences you've had
No matter how good
Regardless how bad
The pages of life turn
So you can learn
Each lesson to be taught
But if you don't learn
Rereading that chapter
Is like taking a long walk
Down the same long road
Same scattered thoughts
Same tattered clothes
When a chapter never ends
It seems to resurface and start all over again
Apply wisdom from pages past
So that chpaters won't last
Any longer
Than it takes to turn the page
Close the curtains on that stage
The play has ended
That lesson's done
Put that chapter behind you
And start a new one.

Edge of Sanity

Hanging myself
From reality's thread
Bombshells of uncertainty
Erupting in my head
Dreams begin where
Nightmare's end
No separation
No pause for resuscitation
Mind's vicious cycle
My soul remains spiteful
Angered by self torture endured
Depleted by feelings insecure
Darkness and light coincide
Fears magnify with closed eyes
Nights' stress fades into the day
Prayers that sleep will fade away
Constant, horrific, pleas unheard
Tears shed in darkness on each deaf word
Questions unanswered by riddles unsolved
Sanity once certain
Now dissolves.

Misdirected

Only a heart
Can bleed love
Stones don't cry
And faceless shadows
Have no fear
Where am I going?
Why am I not there?
No answers for endless questions
No time for unsettled ambition
Constant thoughts
Stimulate emotional pain
Isolated within me
No way to release
No one to understand
Holding my pain
Like cards in my hand
Unplayed
In this game of poker
No partner
And no one else at the table
This life is a fable
A story with an unhappy ending
That keeps my mind bending
Until it reaches full circle
So it can start all over again
Misdirected thoughts
Makes pain a friend.

Disappointment

Disappointed
By failed expectations
The realization
That it's not as easy
As it seems
Life is not a dream
It's hard work
And at times
It hurts
Falling short of your goals
Negativity takes its toll
Performing at a level
Unacceptable
To your standards
How should you handle
This type of feeling
Should you fall to the floor kneeling?
Praying for help
Or should you stand up and try harder
And try to help yourself
We are all disappointed at times
But we must realize
That nothing in this world
Is perfect or without flaw
Even the hardest individuals
At times are soft
So keep trying to reach those goals
'Cause even if you fail
You will still excel
As long as get back up and try again.

The Inner Me

You only see
What I want you to see
You may never see
The inner me
You will never know
What I won't show
You will only know
What you see
On the outside
Unless I feel
I can confide
In you
For the rest
You have no clue
What I go through
Cause I don't feel like
Showing you
You don't need to know
About the pain and disappointments
The insecurities, the lack of enjoyment
You wouldn't understand
The expectations
Both failed and un-attempted
The times my esteem has been put down
Instead of lifted
You couldn't imagine
Through these many years
How many tears
Have been shed
Because of something someone did
Or something someone said
So don't judge me solely
On what you think you see
You only see what I show you
You don't see the inner me.

I Now Realize

Now that the storm is over
The fog lifts
Now I can see clearly
Now realizing that I want you near me
I was wrong for what I said
Those words should have
Never left my mouth
I should have held you
Instead of telling you to get out
My nights without you
Are so cold
This stubborn pride of mine
Is getting old
I'm sorry
I wish you'd pick up the phone
I miss you
Baby
I want you to come home
I now know what you mean to me
I now realize that I lost my queen
I now know what love is
I now know why I shed these tears
I now know what you wanted me to
I now realize baby that I love you.

Pillow Thoughts

On my back
In my bed
Laying in Darkness
With thoughts of your silhouette
Etched
Across the ceiling's pattern
It's been a while
Since you've come through that door
Remember rose petals on the floor
Champagne, Wine
The whole nine
Lord knows
We had a good time
But that was sometime ago
I know
You may have moved on
So I'll stay strong
For the both of us
'Cause if I pick up this phone
You know it's on
An invitation back
For you to reclaim your throne
The passion pit
Will reopen for business
With the quickness
It's a damn shame isn't it?
And you're still apart of my heart
The queen and ruler of my pillow thoughts.

Heartstrings

On my heartstrings
You've played the most
Beautiful melodies
Now
I feel your music
And hear
What you're telling me
This song is so appealing
Undeniably revealing
Of what you've gone through
I sense this is
What you want to do
Playing this song
With such intensity
Can't be wrong
I can tell from your tears
That you wrote this
Over years
A verse here
And another there
For each time I neglected you
Or didn't seem to care
Every time I
Should have listened
When you needed to talk
Those times I should have stayed
But decided to walk
Misunderstandings
And arguments I caused
For no reason
Or no fault of yours
It pains me to listen
But I cannot turn away
I feel what I put you through
In every word you say
All of the insensitive, insecure
And unexplainable things
I now understand
From your last ballad
On my heartstrings.

Since

A thought
A phrase
Echoing into forever
The last impression of you
So true, your love
My heart beats
Irregular
From losing you
Sometime ago
Long before
Maturation
The love penetration
From the glimpse
From that one taste
Of your lips
One simple kiss
We were kids
Compared to now
Wow
I wish I could find you
Somehow
Someway
To say
Hi
Or even
Bye
Or that I've loved you since…
That first kiss
That first glimpse…
Since.
.

Incense

Incense burns
Memories
Of you
In my mind
The aromatic smoke
Fills the room and enters my pores
Like your love
once did a time ago…
With eyes closed
I see you
Clearly
As you
Enter the room
Smelling of sweet perfume
Glowing in anticipation
To greet me
With your love
I smile as I remember
Touching you intimately
As if for the first time
Slowly, gently
Coaxing you near me
As you glide
Into my embrace
Now face to face
I inhale you…
Your pheromones
Fill my lungs
And open my soul
To an erotic playground
The only sound
The rhythm
Of your heart
As the beat slowly quickens
Holding you
Is like…
Holding a dream
Embracing a fantasy
Touching happiness…
Incomprehensible…
As you gaze at me

Incense cont.

With that gentle stare
The moonlight
Etches
Your face
Out of the darkness
Beauty must be your name...

Now immersed
In your presence
I've succumb
To my emotions
I'm lost
Overtaken
By this moment...
By this glimpse...
Of you
As I open my eyes
Still mystified
I realize
The incense is spent..
The last ashes fall
As my mind
Turns a page
Memories
Begin to Fade
Your gone..
But thoughts
Of you
Like the incense aroma
Still remain.

The Fall

Whispers in the wind echo your name
As leaves fall like turned pages in my memories
I see visions of you, of us
Through a clouded glass
Unfocused by pain's past
The panorama of the sunset
Shortens each day's end
As we transition from lovers to friends
Leaving our hot summer nights behind
Searching to find...the exact time
When our stars no longer were aligned
To find exactly our summer's end
And when the fall actually started to begin
Before it became cloudy and constantly overcast
Before the chill from the arctic wind's blast
Before the death of the roses and the grass ceased to grow
Before you stopped loving me...tell me did you know?
Did you see...
The winds of change right before your eyes
The haze appear in our clear blue sky
The leaves as their color began to change
Your attitude when you started to do the same
The love of the man you were to leave behind
And forget that hate has sight...since love is blind
So here I sit
Listening to the wind echo your name
Watching the leaves fall like turned pages in my memories
Seeing you through this clouded glass
Visions of us in the past
So here I sit
In the fall.

Mind Blowing

This crazy
Unfocused daze
Love's powerful haze
Has me blown
I'm open
Swallowed my pride so much
I feel I'm choking
From the way
I feel about you
The only way you could be better
Is if you were two
Love has me entangled
In it's web of passion
Wishing every moment with you
Would last
Eternity…
Sometimes it hurts me
When you're not around
Leaving this hype feenin'
To hear the sound
Of your voice
You're my best and only choice
As a mate
I'm so thankful we decided to date
You are…
My heart's dream
My emotion's desire
Our sparks of passion
Have ignited ecstasy's fire
Leaving me with a mind
Blown away.

Last Night

Last night
I watched you
As you strolled through my dreams
Playing in scenes
My mind created
For you...
Swimming
In a still pool
At the base
Of a tropical waterfall
Soaking up the sun
On a tropical isle
Sometime in the fall
Reading a book
At a small European café'
Enjoying a nice vanilla skim latte'
I watched you as you walked
Through endless fields
As the wind
Blowing through your hair
Gently
Whispered your name
Moving clouds
With your smile
To reveal the endless sky
You laughed and played
Without a thought of tomorrow
Without a thought
At peace with the moment
At peace with life
At peace with the night
That looked down upon you
Your audience
The stars of heaven
Peering down upon you proudly
As if you were their child
Born
From the same magnificence
That created them eons ago...
Last night
I watched

Last Night cont.

You
As you strolled through my dreams
Perfecting scenes
My mind created
for you…
I awake
With a smile on my face
No longer missing you
I spent the entire night
With you
Watching you
Strolling through my dreams
Knowing
Your just a scene…
A dream…
Away.

CREATIVITY STARTS AS A SINGLE THOUGHT...THEN SEEMINGLY TAKES ON A LIFE OF IT'S OWN

Daybreak

A Total black canvas
A still picture
No imagination
Or thought
Only speckled diamonds
Illuminate
Up above
Accented by a crescent star
How far
or how long
Will this
Darkness go?
Until the day
Begins to show
Until the black canvas
Slowly transforms
Waves begin to appear
Although at night we
Can hear them
Swaying rythmically
Against the hull
The outline
The silouhette
Of the terrain
Appears as quickly
As imagination
Rock formations
Mountains, vegetation
Begin to appear
As the sun's illumination
Strengthens
Colors
Are added
To the tapestry
Coinsiding with the deepness
Of the sky's blue tone
The senses moan
While watching the birds
Morning glide
God cannot hide
The magnificience

Daybreak cont.

This day makes
God cannot hide
The magnificience
Of Daybreak.

Circumstance

Some things in life happen
For what appears to be no reason
But so powerful
It changes you
Like the seasons
These occurrences
Don't happen by chance
But due to God driven
Unmistakable circumstance...

During a party I stepped outside
To find myself mesmerized
By this silouhette
Dancing in the moonlight
Like the reflection of an angel
Peering at me on a still pool
Intriguing me to enter
Her world of solitude
Chosen in the midnight air
Inside, the night's festivities rage on
Unaware
Of the portrait Devinci and Michaelangelo
Could not easily recreate or surpass
This unmistakable circumstance
Of one of God's greatest creations
She is young earth
Unpolluted
Beauty's champion
Undisputed
All of nature's majesties manifested
Into one form
Created only by God's own hand
So incredible
That she lacks demand
Because no one is aware
That this type of goddess exists
Pure bliss
Heaven captured in a bottled vision...

Alone she stands
Surrounded by nature's elements

Circumstance cont.

Whose beauty pales in comparison to her own
Peering longingly into the distance
She's mystic
Mysteriously peaceful and serene
The statue of a queen
Standing before her kingdom...

As gravity pulls me near her
I can't help but be entranced
By love's first sight
She senses my presence
And without looking
Extends her hand to greet me
Lovingly
As if she's missed me
And has waited patiently
For my return
Accepting her invitation
I took her hand
And my place
In this kingdom
By her side...

Now
As I stand in her world
As the king of this serene paradise
Peace befalls my mind
I can feel angel's grinning
In the darkness
And the laughter
Of the creatures in the night
Senses magnified
As if I had sight beyond sight...

As I gaze into her eyes
Waterfalls are found in the midst of the sunrise
Stars and mountains are formed at the same time
While Peace and love reign
Over all mankind
Unconditional love
Powers her soul

Circumstance cont.

Supplied from the coal
Found in truth, love, and integrity
She is heavenly
Heaven
All by herself…

We stood
Expressing a world of thoughts
Our lives together
Intertwined hearts
The kingdom we shared
Under God's watchful vision
Her life's purpose
My life's mission
Soaring spiritually above the clouds
Without one word
Being spoken aloud
My queen and I
Stood together
And Conversed for hours…

As the sun began
Its daily return
The queen sadly sighed
And then turned
Toward me
With a tear in her eye
With one last glance, and a kiss
She said goodbye…

Walking away
Into the light of day
She disappeared
Without me knowing her name
With a heart
That beats as pure as mine
The woman I never met
But my love of a lifetime
The future of my life
The blueprint of my wife
Expressed at a glance

Circumstance cont.

As a silhouette in the moonlight?
As I walked away
A smirk fell upon my face
As I knew this meeting was not by chance
God choreographed this dance
As a truly unmistakable circumstance...

Earth

I speak to you
As I see you
Naturally...
As the sun
Rises
Each day
As you awake
Evening's mist rise
Allowing light
To illuminate the tides
The beautiful pools
Found in your eyes
You are unique
Although some come close
To your sculpted formations
And your ivory coast
What separates you
The magma core
Generating heat
Needed
To keep your body warm
Through the winds of change
And those occasional brain...storms
Terrain
Of vegetation, barren lands
Foothills, peaks,
And flatlands
Are found on all extremities
Arms, legs, feet, and hands
The continents
Extending from and including
The motherland
The fertility
Of your soul
Is illustrated in your lifeblood
Coal and oil
Providing nutrients
For your continued growth...
Both
Diamonds and gold
And countless pleasures untold

Earth cont.

Lie within your mine
Time
Your ally
Only enhances the treasures found
Where life's beginning
Resides…
Fluid
Seen on the surface
In your vision
Accounts for most
Of your body's composition
Explaining how you move
So subtle, so smooth
As if you're not in motion at all
But still experiencing
Winter, spring, summer,
And the fall…
The cycle of all life
Occurs within you
Earth
I speak to you
As I see you
Naturally…beautiful.

Another Circumstance

From across
The room
I spotted her
Could this be?
Is that her?...
It's been so long...

Some how
Unknowingly
I know you
From a past life
Another existence
Decades
Or even centuries ago
I can't explain
Knowing everything about you
I can't explain
How your love has guided me this far
Guided me to you
For what seems to be
A second time
I'm almost certain
We were in love once
But the outcome is unclear to me
From the way
You are looking into my eyes
I would say
We never finalized
That chapter
Blank pages
Can still finish this book
Happily ever after
I can tell by your laughter
That I have just spoken
Your exact thoughts...
How do we restart
Without knowing
Where we left off?

This isn't some
Emotional incongestion

Another Circumstance cont.

From love's
Unsuccessful past
Some imaginary
False treasure
Used to pacify
The hopeless romantic
For this moment or
Even on a momentary basis
The honest truth
Since we must face it...
We were meant to be
As sure as
The sun is shining
Behind dark clouds
As sure as
Flowers bloom in May
As sure as
My love
Will make you stay...
Always
Have been my thoughts of you
Daily
Missing you
And wishing for
Your return to me
My heart has burned
During so many cold nights
With thoughts of you
Keeping me warm
As I traveled down the path of
Loners and loneliness
My only wish...
To reunite with
The love of my life
A love that has
Spanned over several lifetimes
A love
That has climbed
Higher than Everest's peak
Gone deeper than
The deepest sea

Another Circumstance cont.

And here you stand
Before me
I'm mesmerized
Entranced by disbelief
Looking into your eyes
I still remember
The tears you cried
The Last time
We parted ways
My heart gave
In the midst
Of your emotional display
Drowning me
In an ocean of your tears
I died that day
A ship sunk
I lay
Emotionally motionless
Stranded
On the bottom of despair
Unrecoverable
No more air
No more reason
To go on
Content with my demise
Without you
On my arm
Now…
Seemingly
Given a second chance
Reuniting with you
In another circumstance
Another chance
At the perfect life
Another chance
With the perfect wife
I stand before you
Despite
All of hell's fury…
My night's of despair
My dried tears

Another Circumstance cont.

My cries in vain
I stand before you
Ready to give you
My last name
Ready to not
Allow you to
Leave me again
Ready to be your
Lover and your friend
My life with you
I'm ready to spend
So take my hand
So we can begin
Our lives together
Once again...

Excuse me miss
Hello
This is going to sound crazy
And a bit cliché but...
You look so familiar...

Another Circumstance.

LOVE SOMEONE THAT WANTS TO LOVE YOU...
NOT SOMEONE WHO'S LOOKING
ONLY FOR SOMEONE TO LOVE...

The Sunrise

Dawn's new day
Follow's night's reign
Over the sky
The moon and stars dance
Like dreams in your mind
Beauty's slumber
Continues to provide
The sunrise I see
Each morning
In your eyes.

At Night I Hear a Whisper...

I hear...
The whisper of your heart
Beating a lullaby
For me to sleep
Under the moon's watchful eye
I hear the whisper
Of your sculpted lips
Telling me love's wish
The hidden pleasures
Comprised within your soul
I hear the whisper
Of your hidden treasures
And your warm body
Nestled next to me
I can hear the whisper
Of your love
Entrancing me
Into an inebriated state
Accented only
By your love's embrace
I hear the whisper
Of your touch
And how I've grown
To love and care for you
So much
I hear the whisper of the night
Remembering the first day
You walked into my life
Our first kiss
Your heart's wish
And all the memories
That we've shared since
At night I hear a whisper...
The whisper...
Of you.

Soon

Serenaded by love's spell
I sleep
Cuddled by the aroma of your perfume...
Soon
I'll be awakened by your tenderness
Your kiss
The sweet taste of your lips
And touch of your fingertips
Gently across my brow
Honestly
I don't know how
Love was made
Before you...
The creation of beauty's perfection
The intension of my passion's affection
I love the sight of you
With each morning's first breath
Inhaling your beauty until there is no air left
Suffocation myself in the love of you...
Soon
In the wake of the stars cloche into the light of day
The sunrise
Will pale in comparison
To the light from your soul
Indescribable
Following slumbers embrace I awake
Yearning to perfect our love
My lips saturating your skin
Is the only way I begin
The infinite ways to express my feelings
As love is made
We are left in a tussle
A tussle of ecstasy
Between you and love's muscle
Until we both reach passion's plateau
That way you know
My love for you is for sure...
Serenaded by love's spell
I sleep
Cuddled by the aroma of your perfume
Waiting to be awakened by your tenderness
Waiting to be awakened...
Soon.

Unforgettable

I still have your image transposed
In the echoes of my mind
Your smile, your kiss
Your every wish
My every desire
To fulfill your every need
You are so remarkable
So incredible
Indescribable
Not possible
With earthly tones
My senses moan
When encountered with the aroma of you
The essence of your womanly being
This heavenly feeling
Can only be…
Unforgettable
Like the breeze that travels the ocean
Relentless and consistent
Steadfast in its pursuit
To reach all shores
Like the beauty of a perfect sky
Cloudless, flawless
So marvelous
Like the look in your eyes
When you are with me
You send me…
Unforgettable
Like feeling joy
For the first time
After years of sorrow
To no longer feel hollow
But to feel fulfilled
Completed
No longer depleted
From life's stresses and worries
To no longer feel hurried
To take my time
And do things right
Like the look in a baby's eyes
Love at first sight…
Unforgettable
As the love I have for you.

Impressions

When your first
Is as important as your last
And the image you leave
Follows you like the shadow you cast
Remembering a smile
Or a simple little laugh
Remembering those you miss
That have faded into the past
There are so many ways
Impressions are made
Both positive and negative
Depending on the day
Life is so precious
When feelings are so true
I hope I made
An unforgettable impression on you
We might cross paths
Again one day
You know I'm sitting here smiling
Cause I'll see you in May
So I hope you think of me
From time to time
And I hope you give me a call
If it's a friend you need to find
I'm quite fond of you
That's plain to see
So it's quite easy to tell
The impression you made on me.

Good Night

As comfort sets in
And sleep begins
I find myself overtaken
By thoughts
Watching you in slumber's embrace
Such a peaceful look on your face
No thoughts of the day
No signs of pain
Just serenity simple and plain
As time moves on
And your slumber grows strong
I know I must depart
On your forehead
I leave love's mark
To bless you through the night
I whisper in your ear
"Good night"
As I blow out the candles
And turn out the lights.

Kiss of a Tear

Looking into your eyes
Since that first time
I always seem to find
Something new
Something so true
Endless characteristics
So beautiful about you
Today
In your eyes
I am surprised
To see the extent of your joy
For me
As your tears kiss my cheek
I stand weak
Now understanding
What it means
To be in love
Uncontrollably, unconditionally
With an angel
Once a stranger
Now my best friend
My beginning
My end
Gazing into your eyes
Unable to speak
I am weak
Feeling the kiss
Of the tears
Running down my cheek.

P.E.E.R.

I'm physically exhausted but emotionally refreshed
Watching my lady rest her head on my chest
The clothes we had on we no longer wear
She's asleep as I run my fingers through her hair
Laying there Reminiscing on the love just made
This is the feeling that I always crave
You know the one that I'm speaking of
When the air is thick with the stench of love
After a love making heat up that is off the charts
When you can feel the beating of your lover's heart
Her fatigue has set in so she takes a nap
Her body is etched in my memory like a map.
I know the routes that will get her there
That comes from true love, not a meaningless affair
Lovemaking is an art and not an act
You can reach a natural high, that's a fact
It's a blissful feeling or something of that kind
The ultimate feeling of PEACE OF MIND.
Moonlight from the window reflecting from her form.
Brings out the true meaning of the quiet storm.
Moments ago, emotions ran fast
Reaching the climax was the ultimate task
The love we shared was easy to show
Our bodies working together to peek and explode
So natural and smooth all at the same time
This is that type of love that lasts a lifetime
You know when both body and mind are involved
And everyday, you feel like you're about fall
In love and love, again… and… again
You can't wait for today to end, and tomorrow to begin
So that you can spend more time with the one you love
Look at her there…as peaceful as a dove.
She's lying there comfortably on my chest
I'm physically exhausted but emotionally refreshed.

Intangible Dreams

Untouched, undiscovered
Uncovered
Imaginary...
Unable to touch
Unable to smell
Unable to taste
But able to feel
Or feel the absence of...
The missing part
The beating heart
The reason to move on
Wake up, live strong
The light in the dark
The fire from the spark
The new start
When the ending can seem so near
The lack of fear
The loss of loneliness
Destruction of despair...
Joy
Happiness
Contentment
Purpose
Excitement
Delight
Caring
Sharing
Involvement
Attachment
Drive
Pleasure
Building
Revealing
And Believing...
The search for...

Love.

The Moment (oftgas)

Nervous Anticipation,
Exhilaration
Heightened senses,
Lost inhibitions
No thoughts
Only hearts
Beating intensively
Into the night
The only sight
Silhouettes
Intertwined
Kisses tasting like wine
Each
Blowing your mind
Further and further
Into the moment…
By this time
Passion
Is clearly defined
Written on your face
Like ancient writings found in caves
Located in far away lands
Translated intimately
By these hands
Moving effortless and smooth over your body
Like warm
Silky bath water
As you get hotter…
Hotter…
And hotter
Approaching the moment…
Skin is exposed
With the removal of clothes
Allowing perspiration
To act as lubrication
As the room temperature begins to climb
Our body heats have now combined
Allowing love and passion
To permeate the air
Allowing my fingers
To run through your hair

The Moment (oftgas) cont.

Both up here...
And...down there
Steadily
So heavenly
In your body
As you reach
The moment...
Of passion's peak
You can no longer speak
Only scream
And moan
As your body explodes
With fists clinched
You try to hold
Onto the moment
And make it last longer
All the while
Your river grows stronger
With intensity and power
This moment
Seems to last an hour
While legs shake
And your canal overflows
Your sea has just
Breached its shores
The rawest and strongest
Of emotions unleashed
Ecstasy in pure form
The moment...
Has been reached.

So Sensual

A chocolate covered
Strawberry
You're the sweetest thing
That I have
Such a taste for...
Levitating around me
As if god's own hand carries you
Your mere touch
Alone
Makes me moan
Having mental orgasms
Off of your skin tone
Why do you tease me so?
A smile
I can see through the phone
When I hear your voice
I have no choice
But to humble myself
Like a servant
Indentured by every syllable
That falls from your tongue
I'm sprung
Only wanting
To endlessly serve you...
Cultured pearl
All world cover girl
Freak of nature
Supernatural
UFO
Unbelievably Fine Object
I can't take it
But I can't stop it
You're the answer
To all of life burning questions
Like...
Who should I fall in love with
Who should I marry
Who do I want to have my kids with
My nerves
Are shot
When I'm around you

So Sensual cont.

Twitching and sweating
As if I'm on trial for my life
Trying not to incriminate myself
And be sentenced to
Life
Without you...
Just so sensual
Like a perfectly
Rippened fruit
So juicy
So sweet
Nurtured by nature
Naturally
Raised by sun's shine
And watched over by moon's glow
The constellations
Spell your name
Angels sing songs
About you
Wishing they had your beauty...
Just so sensual
Like a hot bubble bath
On a winter's night
You take me away
To ecstacy's hideaway
Where passion and pleasure
Go to play
I revert back to childlike ways
When I'm with you
Unsure
Waiting on your every move
To sooth
My thoughts
Hoping you won't leave
Asking you to please
Give me
Just a minute
A moment...of you
Just so sensual...

The Night

Street lights
Casually creep
Through the Blinds
The Night
Has arrived
A world of thoughts
Expressed
In a glance
A peace befalls me
As I watch
Your heart dance
Peering into
Those brown eyes…
Warmth
Expressed
In an embrace
The angelic look
Upon your face
Allows heaven
To reach down
And touch us
If just for this moment…
A kiss goodnight
And a wish
To sleep well
As I escort
The chariot
Carrying you
To sandman's cell
During your slumber
I wonder
If you know
How adorable you are?
The cute way
You fold your legs
Over mine
The affectionate way
You roll over and hold me
From time to time
The phrases you mutter
At times in your dreams

The Night cont.

These are some of the things
That make my heart sing...
Night's progression
Coupled with
The sands of time
Inhibit my euphoria
From lasting a lifetime
The day approaches
As I see
Dawn's first light
The day approaches baby
So I must leave you
For the night.

The Truth

The time we spend together
Is only a fraction of the time
That you are with me
The time we spend together
Is only a fraction of the time
You lift me
You give me joy and happiness
Even when we are apart
Separation
Only enhances
The beating of my heart
And allows me to marinate
In thoughts of you
You are the truth
The light of day
Sunshine to me
In every way
I'm not sure where this will lead
Or if or when it will end
But I'm glad that you
Are in my life
As my lover
And more importantly
My friend…..

If flowers were thoughts
You would sleep in my garden
On a bed of rose petals
Surrounded by God's beautiful creatures
That marvel only at your beauty….

Your Light

Holding you tight
By lunar light
I find that you
Have been seduced by the moon's glow
You too
Reflect the light of the sun
My light
Reflects from your soul
Your glow
In its magnificence
Shines like a beacon
In the darkness
Lighting the path
To your heart.

Fantasy Within a Dream

Life is the Dream
Our love is the Fantasy
The Fantasy
Within the dream
The love
We share
Beyond compare
Only can be explained
By perfect star alignment
Unconfinement
Like a bird
Soaring through the clouds
As a wise "Lima" once said
Happiness exceeding sound
Reality
Escapes
Like the air in a punctured balloon
Every time I'm with you
Leaving me breathless
Euphoric
Even dizzied
By a love high
So potent
Fiends crack
Under the pressure
You're the treasure
The quest
Of my life's dreamlike odyssey
I would choose…
One moment of you
Over life eternal
One taste of your kiss
Over immeasurable riches
One sound of your voice
Over the symphony harmonic
One walk with you
Over rockets traveling supersonic
One ounce of you
Is worth more
Than the earth's weight in Gold
Diamonds, Treasures

Fantasy Within a Dream cont.

Riches untold
Cannot measure
Or equal up to...
The fantasy
Within the dream
The fantasy
Of loving you.

Fantasy in a Dream II (oftgas)

Sleepwalking
In your clutches
Every night
The sight
Of your silhouette
Stretched
Across the bed
The days unclothed dreams
Turn into the night's
Erotic fantasy...
Seeing you, greeting you,
Caressing you, undressing you
Kissing you, hugging you
Licking you, rubbing you
Breasts exposed, panties drop
Past warm, getting hot
Getting hard, getting wet
Temperature rising, start to sweat
Holding you, molding you
Folding you, slow in you
Pleasing me, pleasing you
You scream, I scream too
You need me, I need you
Love this good, can't be true
Can't hold back, love for you
You came hard, I came too
Bodies rest, silhouettes
Lay your head, on my chest...
Fantasies
In daydreams...
Daydreams of
Fantasy.

Just Because...

You ask me why I love you so much
I tell you just because...
Just because you are here
Just because it feels right
Just because god planned it this way...
I think the love is here for a reason...
I love you
As if I'm supposed to
And had no choice in the matter
When god placed you here
In my life
Only he knew
How you would touch my heart
And affect my soul
I know you don't agree
With me feeling this way
But
It is what it is
It is all in God's plan
It is...Just Because of who it is
...YOU...
No other answer
Or explanation necessary
The woman you see in the mirror
Each day
Is the reason why
Just because...you are here in my life
Just because...of the blessing you are
Just because...of how I feel when I'm with you
And how all other's feel who are...
Fortunate enough
To be touched by you
Fortunate enough
To be loved by you
Fortunate enough
To know...
Even a part of you...
You asked me why I love you so much
....Just because it's you.

Sunset and you

As the sun completes it's evening decent
The waves majestic
As they rhythmically massage
The beach below
I can feel your warmth increase
As day fades into night…
Across the horizon
Burnt orange
Is the only light
Fading into the sky's deep blue tapestry
Perfectly
Until only night's dark canvas remains
Love
Pulsates through my veins
As I share this moment with you
Euphoria holds me firmly in her grasp…
I gasp
For one last breath of reality
But I'm gone
Flat lined
Lost
Somewhere between those brown eyes
And that smile
The ocean's tide
The only sound
Love's melody
Played so eloquently
Aloud
By natural harmony
The moon, the stars
The ocean
And you…
My perfect sunset
Come true.